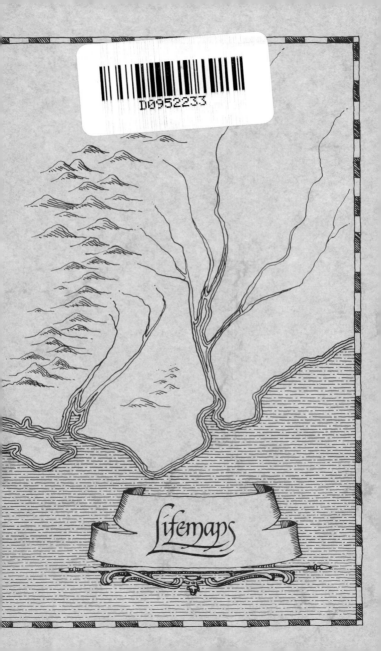

D0952233

Lifemaps

Compassion

Compassion

Showing Care
in a Careless World

Chuck Swindoll

Lifemaps

WORD BOOKS
PUBLISHER
WACO, TEXAS

A DIVISION OF
WORD, INCORPORATED

COMPASSION: SHOWING CARE IN A CARELESS
WORLD

Library of Congress Cataloging in Publication Data

Swindoll, Charles R.
    Compassion: showing care in a careless world.

    (Lifemaps)
    1. Caring—Religious aspects—Christianity.
2. Neighborliness—Religious aspects—Christianity.
I. Title.
BV4647.S9S95   1984   241'.4   84–15358
ISBN 0-8499-0443-9

Unless otherwise indicated, Scripture quotations are
from *The New American Standard Bible,* copyright
© 1960, 1962, 1963, 1968, 1971, 1972, 1973, 1975,
1977 by the Lockman Foundation.

Other Scripture quotations are from the following
sources:
    The Holy Bible: New International Version (NIV),
copyright © 1978 by the New York International
Bible Society.
    The New Testament in Modern English (PHILLIPS),
copyright © 1958, 1960, 1972 by J. B. Phillips.

Printed in the United States of America

And behold, a certain lawyer stood up and put Him to the test, saying, "Teacher, what shall I do to inherit eternal life?" And He said to him, "What is written in the Law? How does it read to you?" And he answered and said, "You shall love the Lord your God with all your heart, and with all your soul, and with all your strength, and with all your mind; and your neighbor as yourself." And He said to him, "You have answered correctly; do this, and you will live." But wishing to justify himself, he said to Jesus, "And who is my neighbor?"

Luke 10:25–29

INTRODUCTION

His dark eyes darted from face to face. His lips were drawn tight across his teeth. His words sounded as if they were propelled from a jet engine. There was no monkey business with this coach. He was tough, determined as a steer in a blizzard. His job was a simple one—to build a championship team out of a rag-tag bunch of discouraged rookies and tired "has-beens." But Vince Lombardi didn't know the word *can't*. And he refused to complicate a game that, when boiled down to the basics, consisted of blocking, tackling, running, passing, catching—all to be done with abandon.

As he often said, "You do all those things right, you win. It's a matter of the basics. You gotta concentrate on the basics."

I will never forget this man's words to his beloved Green Bay Packers on one occasion when he emphasized the basics. There they sat in a heap, tons of massive humanity hanging on the words of one man. Holding the pigskin high in the air, he shouted, "Okay, gentlemen . . . today we go back to the basics. You guys, look at this. *This* is a FOOTBALL!"

I smile every time I recall that true story. There sat seasoned men, some of whom had played the game more than twenty years. They knew the playbook better than they knew their own children's names! And here's this coach with the audacity to tell them, "This is a football!"

That's like the conductor of the Philadelphia Philharmonic leaning over to the concert master, pointing to the score and saying, "This is a half note." It's like a student handing the librarian a copy of the latest best seller with the comment, "This is a book." Or like pointing to an infant's underclothing and saying to a mother of young twins, "This is a diaper!" I mean, how basic can you get?

There are times that I am tempted to stand up in front of a group of Christians and say "Ladies and gentlemen, it's time to go back to basics." And having said that, I would point to an individual in the audience or someone on the platform and say, "*This* is a neighbor!"

What the ball is to the game, what the music note is to the symphony, what the book is to the library . . . a neighbor is to Christianity. When that realization sinks in, I am convinced it will revolutionize our whole perspective regarding evangelism, world missions, the church, even the home.

High-powered and often high-priced Christian strategists invest long hours and valuable energy mapping out a plan to "reach the world." A philosophy is hammered out. Methods are thought through. Gifted men and women are educated, screened, trained, and dispatched. Crusades are conducted. Clinics and hospitals are built. Translations are completed and published. Prayers are offered. Monies are raised and spent. All this is fine. It's essential. It's commendable. And God honors much of it. But it is *not* basic. Getting across the seas is not the primary goal of Christianity—not even getting across the States.

Our primary job is getting across the street. It's going next door. It's showing Christ's love to that person at the desk next to us at school or to those with whom we rub shoulders at the office or in the shop.

This book is about that individual whom the Bible calls our "neighbor." It's about how to keep from turning him or her off . . . how to create within that person's mind a curiosity, even a longing, to know the only One who can give life meaning and hope. It's really about that single, rare ingredient that causes Christianity to have credibility, the link that connects us with our neighbors—compassion.

But I should warn you ahead of time. The stuff that follows is explosive. Unless you're ready to be jolted from your comfortable and cozy world where the womb of theory protects you from a life of reality, you really don't want to pursue this subject. Compassion may seem safe. It may even have an appealing ring to it. But it has been known to start revolutions. And if you become addicted, nothing else satisfies. You'll be different. You'll be hooked for the rest of your life—like someone else I know . . . Christ.

Chuck Swindoll
Fullerton, California

Showing Care
in a Careless World

*"Truly I say to you, to the extent that
you did it to one of these brothers of
Mine, even the least of them, you did
it to Me."*

Matthew 25:40

DIALOGUE ON THE STREET

Okay, so you're willing to take the plunge. Good for you. In order to understand what compassion means to Christianity, let's start in the first century, with the Person of Jesus Christ, on the street where real men and women heard His words and watched Him work.

On that particular street, among the crowd of onlookers, was a lawyer. Like all lawyers he was trained to think, to examine the evidence, to probe for the flaw, to ask the hard questions. Having observed the scene sufficiently, the attorney decided to ask a question. It was to the point.

> "Teacher, what shall I do to inherit eternal life?" (Luke 10:25).

What a question! In my twenty-five years of ministry, I could count on both hands the times I've been asked that question so directly and would have fingers left over. I'm telling you, I would love to answer that question.

But the beautiful thing about Jesus' answer was that it was so profound, so unexpected—not the predictable pat answer you might expect from somebody today. As a matter of fact, His answer was actually another question.

> "What is written in the Law? How does it read to you?" (Luke 10:26).

Perhaps Jesus had noticed something the man was wearing. In those days the strict scribes (first-century lawyers) wore little leather pouches on their wrists into which they placed selected statements from the *Torah*. These pouches were called "phylacteries." Jesus may have seen the man's phylacteries and realized that he had within them the very answer for which he was searching. Maybe He simply wanted the man to do further thinking before evaluating the answer. Whatever, the lawyer's answer was swift and succinct.

> "You shall love the Lord your God with all your heart, and with all your soul, and with all your strength, and with all your mind; and your neighbor as yourself" (Luke 10:27).

Drawing his answer from two sections of the Law, the attorney wasted no time. His response was right on target.

No one from the crowd interrupted the interchange. I imagine it was as if the scribe and the Savior were alone on the street, their eyes locked on each other . . . both concentrating on the subject; neither allowing his mind to wander. Onlookers must have wondered what the Nazarene's response would be to such a quick and concise answer. And they probably breathed a sigh of relief when they heard—

"You have answered correctly."

But I'm certain the next statement turned all eyes back toward the scribe, almost as if the crowd were following a verbal tennis match.

"Do this and you will live."

Suddenly, the ball was back in the lawyer's court. And if I know anything about lawyers, they don't like balls in their court! They much prefer serving to returning. I can't help but wonder if the man didn't squirm a bit. No doubt, the "You have answered correctly" part was nice to hear. It was the "Do this" comment that forced his hand.

Notice that Dr. Luke adds an insightful tidbit before recording the lawyer's next volley.

But wishing to justify himself, he said to Jesus, "And who is my neighbor?" (v. 29).

This time the lawyer's question is borne out of a defensive spirit. The man felt the screws tightening. He was under the gun to produce. In effect, Jesus had said, "You want eternal life? You are interested in the life I'm offering that will be distinctively different? Then you should know up front that it will have a drastic effect on you, both vertically (with God) and horizontally (with your neighbor)." The vertical part he could fake. (Who could ever produce the evidence that he failed at loving the Lord his God with all his heart and mind?) But the horizontal? When it came to loving his neighbor—ah, there was the rub!

So, being a good attorney, he picked

at terms. He understood the sentence, but there was that nagging word *neighbor—Who, pray tell, is one's neighbor? Is it just the fella next door? Or two doors away? Or down around the corner? What if his skin is black? What if she speaks a different language from mine? Does she qualify as my neighbor? You see, Jesus, that's a pretty vague word.*

The dialogue in Luke 10 reminds me of a true story I heard theologian Carl F. H. Henry tell as he spoke to a group of radio broadcasters. The late Dr. Reinhold Niebuhr (no pun intended) decided to write out his theological position, stating exactly where he stood philosophically—his credo. Being the profound thinker he was (and a bit verbose), it took him many sheets of paper to express himself. Upon completion of his masterwork, he realized it was in need of being read and evaluated by a mind much more practical than his own. He bundled up

the material and sent it to a minister
whom he knew had a practical mind and
a pastoral "heart."

With great pains the clergyman
sweated through this ream of paper,
trying desperately to grasp the meaning.
When he finally finished, he worked up
the nerve to write a brief yet absolutely
candid note in reply. It read:

My dear Dr. Niebuhr:

I understand every word you have
written, but I do not understand *one*
sentence.[1]

I suggest that the first century
attorney had the opposite problem. He
understood the sentence, but he had
trouble with the word *neighbor*. So he
asked, "And who is my neighbor?"

WHO IS MY NEIGHBOR?

Who is my neighbor? Great question! If I live to be 150 years old, I will still be impressed with the way Jesus answered the lawyer's question. Rather than digging into the etymology of the term or rebuking the guy for being defensive, He simply told a story. As is true of all the stories Jesus told, this one appeared harmless, almost childlike, but behind it lay a vast network of implications.

The short story caught the attention of the lawyer because its setting was familiar territory. Read it as if for the first time.

Jesus replied and said, "A certain man was going down from Jerusalem to Jericho; and he fell among robbers, and they stripped him and beat him, and went off leaving him half dead. And by chance a certain priest was going down on that road, and when he saw him, he passed by on the other side. And likewise a Levite also, when he came to the place and saw him, passed by on the other side. But a certain Samaritan, who was on a journey, came upon him; and when he saw him, he felt compassion, and came to him, and bandaged up his wounds, pouring oil and wine on them; and he put him on his own beast, and brought him to an inn, and took care of him. And on the next day he took out two denarii and gave them to the innkeeper and said, 'Take care of him; and whatever more you spend, when I return, I will repay you' " (Luke 10:30–35).

The Setting

Between Jerusalem and Jericho stretched twenty miles of bad road. Not only did it drop twenty-three hundred feet in elevation, but it was a notorious "alley" where thieves, rapists, and other criminal types hung out. The twists and turns in the rugged road provided them places to surprise their victims as well as carry out their vicious crimes.

I don't know of a metropolis in America that doesn't have a few places that are unsafe to travel alone. Some urban areas have a few streets; others like New York City, Chicago, Houston, and Los Angeles have sprawling sections from which the general public stays away. In such neighborhoods the only time it's safe to go for a walk is when the policemen are having their annual parade—and you are marching in it!

This road was like that. Every Jew for miles around knew it. So when Jesus started His story with the account of a man who traveled that road, everybody listening, no doubt, anticipated that trouble was certain.

The Victim

Predictably, the man was assaulted, stripped, beaten, and left to die beside the road. According to Jesus' words, they "went off leaving him half dead."

Before going on, let me remind you of something you may have already forgotten. This story grows out of a question the lawyer asked, "Who is my neighbor?" Interestingly, we are never told the origin of the victim. We assume he was a Jew, perhaps a Jerusalem resident, but we have no idea as to the specific location of his home. He is called merely "a certain man"—nothing more.

Two Fellow Travelers

Three people are identified as those who were traveling the same road, who saw the man in his desperate situation. Admittedly, none of the three knew the victim. Let's consider the first two.

The first was "a certain priest." We

learn from the story that he was on the road and that he saw the man. But when he saw him, he deliberately walked away from him. He "passed by on the other side."

We can understand. Ministers are busy people. Schedules to keep, deadlines to meet, sermons to prepare. And who could blame the priest for being somewhat afraid of falling into a trap? Furthermore, if we got technical about it, the priest could excuse his actions by claiming that he was not to be "ceremonially contaminated" by touching someone in that condition. After all, we need to keep our equilibrium and not get "carried away" by every person in need. Sound familiar?

Second, there came along a Levite. Perhaps we'd be in the ball park if we thought of him as an assistant minister discipled by the priest. He, too, was terribly involved in his work. People were waiting, there were programs to plan, functions to arrange, certainly a similar set of ceremonial requirements to fulfill. So we shouldn't be surprised to notice that he also "passed by on the other side" when he caught a glance of the bleeding victim. "Poor guy . . . if only I had time to stop."

Before moving on to the third, let me mention an actual event that occurred on the campus of an evangelical seminary, the very grounds where future ministers were in training. A Greek class was given an assignment to study Luke 10:25–37—the same Good Samaritan story we are considering. These young theologs were to do an in-depth analysis of the biblical text, observing and commenting on all the major terms and syntactical factors worth mentioning. Each student was to write his own translation after having done the work on his commentary.

As is true in most language classes, a couple or three of the students cared more about the practical implications of the assignment than its intellectual stimulation. The morning the work was to be turned in, these three teamed up and carried out a plan to prove their point. One volunteered to play the part of an alleged victim. They tore his shirt and trousers, rubbed mud, catsup, and other realistic-looking ingredients across his "wounds," marked up his eyes and face so he hardly resembled himself, then placed him along the path that led from the dormitory to the Greek classroom. While the other two hid and watched, he groaned and writhed, simulating great pain.

Not one student stopped. They walked around him, stepped over him, and said different things to him. But nobody stooped over to help. What do you want to bet their academic work was flawless . . . and insightful . . . and handed in on time?

This incident always reminds me of a scripture that penetrates the surface of our intellectual concerns.

This is how we know what love is: Jesus Christ laid down his life for us. And we ought to lay down our lives for our brothers. If anyone has material possessions and sees his brother in need but has no pity on him, how can the love of God be in him? (1 John 3:16–17, NIV).

It also reminds me of a scene out of *Winnie the Pooh.* Even though the little creatures are imaginary, we can see ourselves in them. This particular scenario reveals how downright insensitive we often are.

Pooh Bear is walking along the river bank. Eeyore, his stuffed donkey friend, suddenly appears floating downstream . . . on his back of all things, obviously troubled about the possibility of drowning.

Pooh calmly asks if Eeyore had fallen in. Trying to appear in complete control, the anguished donkey answers, "Silly of me, wasn't it." Pooh overlooks his friend's pleading eyes and remarks that

Eeyore really should have been more careful.

In greater need than ever, Eeyore politely thanks him for the advice (even though he needs action more than he needs advice). Almost with a yawn, Pooh Bear notices, "I think you are sinking." With that as his only hint of hope, drowning Eeyore asks Pooh if he would mind rescuing him. So, Pooh pulls him from the river. Eeyore apologizes for being such a bother, and Pooh, still unconcerned, yet ever so courteous, responds, "Don't be silly . . . you should have said something sooner." [2]

I find it absolutely amazing how closely that episode reflects the world of real people in real need! How many Eeyores there are, soaked to the ears and about to drown, yet we keep ourselves safely separated with nice-sounding questions and always courteous remarks! We'll even say, "Give me a call if you need me." Honestly now, when's the last time someone in need gave you a call?

Do you really believe that will ever happen? And even if the person worked up the courage to call, would you be serious about helping? We learn early how to say all the right words, yet deep down mean *none* of them.

One Compassionate Samaritan

The average citizen may not really care about the other fellow, but there are a few marvelous exceptions like this third man Jesus mentioned. Before we take a look at this compassionate traveler, it is important to realize that his race and heritage play a significant part in Jesus' story. Bluntly, he was a half-breed. True Jews so hated the Samaritans that they refused all contact with them. They literally hated to have Samaritan dust soil their sandals. If a Judean down South planned to visit Galilee up North, since Samaria lay smack dab in the middle of that journey, they went *around* it, rather than through it.

While explaining that recently, I drew an analogy from our own United States, saying that would be comparable to a Texan traveling to Kansas, but going around Oklahoma. After the meeting I was cornered by three massive men, each well over 250 pounds and not one shorter than six feet, four inches. They were Oklahoma Sooners and they informed me (jokingly), "We jus' wanna make it clear that we ain't got no Samaritans in Oklahoma!" I smiled as I drove home that night, realizing that not even today are Samaritans free of prejudice! But then my thoughts grew serious as I reflected on Jesus' story.

You can be sure that when the lawyer heard Jesus mention that "a certain Samaritan" was on the Jericho road, the hair on the back of his neck probably stood up. The Lord knew what He was saying. Again, remember that He was answering "Who is my neighbor?" By now it was becoming obvious to everyone that the answer must not be connected to geography . . . or race . . . or lifestyle. Difficult as it must have been for the attorney to accept it, he was forced to hear that the Jewish victim was helped by the Samaritan stranger.

Do you recall the difference between the Samaritan's response and that of the first two travelers? All three "saw" the one who had been stripped, beaten, and abandoned, but he alone "felt compassion" for the man. Compassion— that was what set the Samaritan apart from the other two. It was the connecting link, the magnet that drew him to the victim.

The message is still the same. Invariably, compassion says, "Get involved. Reach out. Risk. You can't ignore this person's needs. You care too much to walk away." Another New Testament writer sees compassion as that which makes Christianity authentic. Like a one-sided coin, faith without works is counterfeit. Listen to the way James says it.

Now what use is it, my brothers, for a man to say he "has faith" if his actions do not correspond with it? Could that sort of faith save anyone's soul? If a fellow man or woman has no clothes to wear and nothing to eat, and one of you say[s], "Good luck to you, I hope you'll keep warm and find enough to eat," and yet give[s] them nothing to meet their physical needs, what on earth is the good of that? (James 2:14–16, PHILLIPS).

Obviously, the Samaritan's faith was authentic. His compassion went to work. Consider his genuine concern.

- He came to him.
- He bandaged up his wounds.
- He poured oil and wine on them.
- He put him on his own beast.
- He brought him to an inn.
- He stayed the night, taking care of him.
- He picked up the tab . . . he even promised to return and pay whatever other expenses might be incurred.

In concluding His story, Jesus no doubt peered intently into the lawyer's eyes as He asked the crucial question: "Which of these three do you think proved to be a neighbor to the man who fell into the robbers' hands?"

Wait a minute. That's a different question from the one that led into the story of the Good Samaritan. The original question was "Who is my neighbor?" By looking toward the other person, it allowed the one asking the question to be protected and safe as he searched the horizon for that special individual who qualified as "my neighbor." Refusing to fan an irrelevant flame, Jesus shifted the emphasis so that the question worth considering at the end of the story is not "Which person qualifies as *my* neighbor?" but "What kind of neighbor *am I?*" You see, *that* question points the finger in the other direction—in the lawyer's direction, in your direction, in my direction.

To use today's terms, not "Is my neighbor really lost and therefore needy?" but "Is my neighbor's *neighbor*—namely, me—really saved and therefore compassionate?"

Thankfully, the lawyer got the point. His answer was right on. Which one proved to be a neighbor? "The one who showed mercy toward him." Jesus' answer has come full circle. Before the story He had told the scribe, "Do this and you will live" (Luke 10:28). He now says virtually the same thing, "Go and do the same" (v. 37). Our greatest need is not to hold back until we locate some special individual who qualifies as *the* one. It is to realize that there are needs all around us, each one awaiting a tangible demonstration of compassion, and that involvement proves that we possess eternal life.

STRAIGHT TALK ABOUT COMPASSION

Let's get specific. It is doubtful that there is anything more basic, more Christlike, and therefore more Christian than compassion.

For some strange reason we've missed this, especially we who are evangelicals. In place of compassion we have deliberately substituted *information*. Somehow we have determined that knowledge will heal wounds. We have convinced ourselves that facts are what the hurting soul really needs. Good truth, to be sure, but little more.

When did we buy into such heresy? Where, pray tell, do we find Christ modeling such a thing? Don't misunderstand, biblical truth is important, doctrinal knowledge is valuable, but it comes later . . . after mercy has won a hearing, after compassion has prepared the soil into which truth can take root.

If I could put this entire book into one sentence, it would be:

OTHERS WILL NOT CARE HOW MUCH WE KNOW UNTIL THEY KNOW HOW MUCH WE CARE.

Read that again and again and again. Say it aloud. Write it in the frontispiece of your Bible. Mention it to a friend. Pass it on in a letter. But most of all, put it to the test. And that requires an active reaching out beyond our safe and protective wall. But reach out we must.

As one authority puts it:

If I just do my thing and you do yours, we stand in danger of losing each other

and ourselves. . . . We are fully ourselves
only in relation to each other; the I
detached from a Thou disintegrates. I do
not find you by chance; I find you by an
active life of reaching out.[3]

Insightful Perception

People with compassion reach out
because they perceive needs. And most
needs are not nearly so obvious as the
Jericho road victim. Those we bump up
against may be equally "stripped,
beaten, and abandoned," but much of
it is kept inside—behind walls of
pseudosecurity, hidden beneath masks
that smile and say "Fine, I'm just fine."
But more often than not, there are
lurking fears and fragile feelings of
insecurity behind those masks.
Compassionate-Samaritan types aren't
fooled by such surface smoke screens.
They refuse to walk away mouthing the
glib yet popular farewell, "Have a nice
day." One author has been honest and

vulnerable enough to speak for many with these penetrating statements of admission.

Don't be fooled by me. Don't be fooled by the face I wear. I wear a mask. I wear a thousand masks—masks that I am afraid to take off; and none of them are me.

Pretending is an art that is second nature to me, but don't be fooled. For my sake, don't be fooled. I give the impression that I am secure, that all is sunny and unruffled within me as well as without; that confidence is my name and coolness is my game, that the water is calm and I am in command; and that I need no one. But don't believe me, please. My surface may seem smooth, but my surface is my mask, my ever-varying and ever-concealing mask.

Beneath lies no smugness, no complacence. Beneath dwells the real me in confusion, in fear, in aloneness. But I hide that. I don't want anybody to know it. I panic at the thought of my weakness and fear being exposed. That's why I frantically create a mask to hide behind— a nonchalant, sophisticated facade—to help me pretend, to shield me from the glance that knows. But such a glance is precisely my salvation, my only salvation, and I know it. That is, if it's followed by acceptance; if it's followed by love.

It's the only thing that can liberate me from myself, from my own self-built prison wall, from the barriers I so painstakingly erect. It's the only thing that will assure me of what I can't assure myself—that I am really something. . . .

Who am I, you may wonder. I am someone you know very well. I am every man you meet. I am every woman you meet. I am every child you meet. I am right in front of you. Please . . . love me.[4]

Compassionate people understand and accept those words. They possess "the glance that knows" as well as the love and acceptance mask-wearing strugglers need in order to feel sufficiently secure to drop their guard. They are truly remarkable and rare individuals.

Personal Illustration

One of the finest examples of Christlike compassion I have ever known is my older brother Orville. He is a veteran missionary in Buenos Aires . . . a man of great intellect, yet a heart for God like few people I have ever known. Among my earliest memories from our home, I distinctly recall awaking in the middle of the night and seeing Orville on his knees in prayer.

You may not like to read this, but I resented his close (and, in my opinion at the time, *fanatical*) relationship with God. I remember thinking, *What a drag. Why couldn't I have a "normal" brother who played football, who lettered in several sports, who liked to fish and hunt? How come I'm stuck with this teenaged monk instead of a red-blooded all-American?* I have long since come to realize just how valuable Orville's life really was—and is—but back then I wrestled deeply with such questions. To me, he was just too much.

Let me interject that he, my sister Luci, and I were raised by an extremely pragmatic father. Say what you like about the walk of faith, my dad was too functional and practical to get very excited about totally trusting God. Don't get me wrong, he was a Christian, but he didn't buy into any extreme view of Christianity. "It's okay to talk about faith and depending on the Lord, but God gave you a brain, so use it. He also gave you arms and muscles, so be responsible." I suppose the statement "There ain't no free spiritual lunch" says it best. He believed in hard work and taking care of what you owned and protecting yourself from the nuts and rip-offs. "Don't be foolish. Fight laziness.

If you've got shoes, keep 'em shined. If you own a car, keep it clean. Don't slam the door. Make your bed. Mow the grass. Don't pick up hitchhikers. Choose your friends carefully. Never mess around with guys who drink, fast girls, total strangers (especially ex-cons), people who borrow money, or loud-mouthed, fast-talking salesmen." You've got the picture. But Orville always had trouble when those "rules" bumped up against the walk of faith. Allow me to jump ahead a few years.

When my brother was mustered out of the Navy, he drove from the Great Lakes area toward Houston. While en route, he picked up a stranger on the road somewhere in Kansas. It was cold and windy, so the hitchhiker was mighty pleased to take a seat in a warm car. It wasn't long before the two of them got on the subject of spiritual things. The man had led a rugged life. In fact, he had recently been released from prison. The black backdrop of his past provided

Orville with a perfect canvas upon which to paint the beautiful message of Christ's death for sinners and his offer of forgiveness and eternal life to all who believe.

As you'd expect, my brother's winsome, personable approach, mixed with his authentic compassion for the man in need, proved irresistible. The man quietly and humbly took the gift and became a "new creature in Christ."

By the time the two of them reached central Oklahoma, the stranger announced that he was near his home. Here is where he got off. As he opened the door, the wintry blast filled the car.

"Where's your coat?" asked Orville.

"Well, I don't have one . . . but I'll be fine."

"Wait a minute," Orville interrupted. With that, my brother reached back into his seabag and dug out his Navy pea jacket. You remember that dark blue, double-breasted, big-collar government issue every sailor wore on cold days. He tossed the jacket toward the stranger, smiled, and said, "Here's your new coat." Shivering, the man buttoned it up, then leaned through the door and, with great sincerity, said, "In all my life I've never met anyone like you. How can I ever thank you enough?"

Meanwhile, back in Houston, my dad is awaiting the arrival of his older son. Clipboard in hand. Ready to check off the seabag supplies. Was he in for a surprise! I was only a teenager at the time, but it has been indelibly imprinted in my museum of memories.

"Eight pairs of socks?"

"Check. Eight pairs."

"Three caps?"

"Check. Three caps."

"Six white T-shirts?"

"Check. Six T-shirts."

"Eight pairs of skivvies?"

"Check. Eight pairs."

"Two pairs of shoes?"

"Check. Two pairs."

"One pea jacket?"

"Uh . . . well . . ."

"Where's the jacket?"

"It's not here, Dad." (My brother always had a great grasp of the obvious.)

"I can see that! Where is it?"

"Well, it's somewhere in central Oklahoma."

"Did you lose it?"

"No, actually, I *gave* it away."

"To whom?"

Swallowing hard, he took a deep breath and stated with calm confidence, "Dad, I gave it to a hitchhiker that I picked up in Kansas. He had just gotten out of prison and he didn't have a coat, so I gave him mine."

One incredible space of silence transpired as the two of them locked eyes. Finally, my father leaned across the kitchen table, cleared his throat, and responded, "You know, Orville, I haven't understood you for a long time." To which my brother replied—standing about three inches from Dad's nose—

"No, Dad . . . and I don't think you ever will."

I learned a never-to-be-forgotten lesson that afternoon. Compassionate people are often hard to understand. They take risks most people would never take. They give away what most would cling to. They reach out and touch when most would hold back with folded arms. They don't usually operate on the basis of human logic or care very much about rules of safety. Their caring brings them up close where they feel the other person's pain and do whatever is necessary to demonstrate true concern. An arm's-length "be warmed and be filled" comment won't cut it. As one understanding soul expressed it:

Compassion is not a snob gone slumming. Anybody can salve his conscience by an occasional foray into knitting for the spastic home. Did you ever take a real trip down inside the broken heart of a friend? To feel the sob of the soul—the raw, red crucible of emotional agony? To have this become almost as much yours as that of your soul-crushed neighbor? Then, to sit down with him—and silently weep? This is the beginning of compassion.[5]

There will be no whistles or loud applause. Crawling into that "raw, red crucible" is no pastime for glory hogs. In fact, the best acts of compassion will never be known by the masses. Nor will there be fat sums of money dumped into your lap because you are committed to being helpful. It is only once in a blue moon that a Mother Teresa will be awarded the Nobel Peace Prize. Normally, it will be acts of mercy done in obscurity with no thought of monetary gain.

A war correspondent paused long enough to watch a nun as she unwrapped a wounded soldier's leg. Gangrene had set in. The stench from the pus and blood was so repulsive that he turned away as he mumbled under his breath, "I

wouldn't do that for a million bucks."
She glanced up and replied, "Neither
would I."

Would you? Is that what it would take?
Ruth Harms Calkin touches a sensitive
spot in all of us as she wonders—

You know, Lord, how I serve You
With great emotional fervor
In the limelight.
You know how eagerly I speak for You
At a women's club.
You know how I effervesce when I promote
A fellowship group.
You know my genuine enthusiasm
At a Bible study.

But how would I react, I wonder
If You pointed to a basin of water
And asked me to wash the calloused feet
Of a bent and wrinkled old woman
Day after day,
Month after month,
In a room where nobody saw
And nobody knew.[6]

Compassion usually calls for a willingness to spend oneself in humility on behalf of unknowns in a context of obscurity. How few there are in our fast-paced, get-rich-quick society who say to such a task, "Here am I, use me." But if I may return to my opening remarks, there is nothing more basic, nothing more Christian. If God's people are to be living examples of one thing, that thing ought to be—it must be—compassion. I could not agree more with the late great preacher John Henry Jowett. When he was asked what he would emphasize if he had his life to live over, with obvious emotion he replied, "I would major on compassion and comfort."

CONCLUSION: A PENETRATING THOUGHT

There are times in my life when I am seized with a scene from Scripture. Ever had that happen to you? Not too long ago it happened again to me. It was late at night. I clicked the last light out and lowered my head onto the pillow. Outside was a clear, deep blue sky with stars shining brightly through the crisp night air. It was one of those nights when my body was tired but my mind wouldn't shift into neutral. I had been reading in the Gospel of Matthew and the scene kept passing in review. The night sky aided my imagination, since one day in the future this scene will actually transpire in space . . . out there where only the stars now reside.

I blinked nervously as the words burned their way into the window pane. I wanted to reach over and feel the inspired etching.

But when the son of Man comes in His glory, and all the angels with Him, then He will sit on His glorious throne. And all the nations will be gathered before Him; and He will separate them from one another, as the shepherd separates the sheep from the goats; and He will put the sheep on His right, and the goats on the left (Matt. 25:31–33).

What an incredible moment that will be, I mused. *All of humanity will be gathered at that epochal hour before the Savior's throne—sheep and goats alike, separated and awaiting those eternal words from His lips.* I swallowed hard, blinked again, and forced myself to think

through those final words to the sheep.
Do you remember them?

> Then the King will say to those on His
> right, "Come, you who are blessed of My
> Father, inherit the kingdom prepared for
> you from the foundation of the world. For
> I was hungry, and you gave Me something
> to eat; I was thirsty, and you gave Me
> drink; I was a stranger, and you invited
> Me in; naked, and you clothed Me; I was
> sick, and you visited Me; I was in prison,
> and you came to Me" (Matt. 25:34–36).

They will be awestruck, according to
the biblical text. They will stare in
amazement as they attempt to unravel
the mystery of their Lord's being hungry
and thirsty . . . a stranger . . . one who
needed clothing as well as having been
in prison and being visited by them.
Unable to contain their curiosity, they
will burst forth in one voice with:

> "Lord, when did we see You hungry, and
> feed You, or thirsty, and give You drink?

And when did we see You a stranger, and invite You in, or naked, and clothe You? And when did we see You sick, or in prison, and come to You?" (Matt. 25:37–39).

His answer blew me away as I lay there staring out the window. I was momentarily stunned with the impact of His words. Take the time to study His answer slowly and thoughtfully.

And the King will answer and say to them, "Truly I say to you, to the extent that you did it to one of these brothers of Mine, even the least of them, you did it to Me" (Matt. 25:40).

Talk about penetrating!
Do you realize what He is saying? The Person named Jesus Christ, our King and sovereign Lord, will one day invite His own into His glorious kingdom, because the authenticity of their faith was demonstrated by the way they treated "the least of these My brothers." Please

note that the emphasis is on "the least"—
the obscure, the broken, the battered,
the unknowns . . . not the celebrities
. . . not the big names . . . not the
whole, the well-healed, the prima
donnas, but the *least*.

Authoress Gloria Hope Hawley, a lady
in our church who is the mother of two
retarded "children" (both of them are
now grown but still live at home), slipped
the following paraphrase into my hand.
It pretty well sums up the idea.

. . . and He said, "I was afflicted with
cerebral palsy and you listened to my
faltering speech and gently held my
flailing hands; I was born a Down's
syndrome child and you welcomed me
into your church. I was retarded and your
love reached out to me." And the people
said, "Lord, when did we see you with
cerebral palsy and listen to you, and when
were you born with Down's syndrome or
retarded?" He said, "In that you did it to
the least of these my people, you did it
to me."

Christianity doesn't get more basic than that. It is seeing value in, and loving and caring for, and reaching out to, and spending time with "the least of these." In a word, it is compassion. Those words in Matthew's account are saying in a nutshell: If Christianity is Christ and if Christ is compassion . . . then Christianity's finest expression is compassion. Those were my thoughts that starlit night and they remain my thoughts to this day. I couldn't agree more with Jeremy Jackson who wrote:

> It is a fair rule of thumb that only that love of neighbor which can also draw people to Christ is truly a reflection of that love for God which is its source.[7]

Do you want Christ to be seen in your life? Do you long to have an effective ministry with eternal dimensions in the lives of others? Do you desire to hear King Jesus' voice some future day inviting you to enjoy the rewards of His kingdom with Him? Who doesn't? Then I suggest that you decide now to be different. To risk reaching, without waiting for an invitation to help. Decide now that you are going to invest more of your energy and time on those stripped, beaten, and abandoned individuals. They will seldom tell you, but they need to feel His touch through your hands. They are too shy or too proud or too humiliated or too afraid to ask for help, even though they know they're not going to make it on their own. When you allow your compassion to flow freely, you won't need a personal invitation . . . but, like the Samaritan, you'll stop, stoop, and serve.

Will it be costly? Yes, sometimes. Notice what author Michael Quoist has to say:

> Lord, why did you tell me to love all
>   men as my brothers?
> I have tried, but I come back to you
>   frightened.

Lord, I was so peaceful at home, so
  comfortably settled.
It was well-furnished, and I felt so cozy.
I was alone—I was at peace.
Sheltered from the wind and the rain,
  kept clean.[8]

Our God wants to dislodge us from our
comfortable, smug existence, to move us
to mingle with our needy brothers, to
stir us to touch those we might otherwise
shun. An anonymous poet expressed the
challenge well.

Love has a hem to her garment
  That trails in the very dust;
It can reach the stains of the streets
    and lanes,
  And because it can, it must.

Since when did the Christian hold
back because something was costly? Or
because it brought discomfort? That
kind of restraint was the very trap the
people in Isaiah's day fell into, leaving
them smug and complacent, massaging

a lifeless religion that looked and sounded orthodox, but in actuality it lacked substance. The prophet disturbed them (prophets always do!) by reminding them of their primary task as the people of God.

Is this not the fast which I chose,
To loosen the bonds of wickedness,
To undo the bands of the yoke,
And to let the oppressed go free,
And break every yoke?
Is it not to divide your bread with
the hungry,
And bring the homeless poor into
the house;
When you see the naked, to cover
him;
And not to hide yourself from your
own flesh?
Then your light will break out like
the dawn,
And your recovery will speedily
spring forth;
And your righteousness will go
before you;
The glory of the Lord will be your
rear guard.
Then you will call, and the Lord
will answer;
You will cry, and He will say, "Here
I am."
If you remove the yoke from your
midst,

*The pointing of the finger, and
speaking wickedness,
And if you give yourself to the
hungry,
And satisfy the desire of the afflicted,
Then your light will rise in
darkness,
And your gloom will become like
midday.
And the Lord will continually
guide you,
And satisfy your desire in scorched
places,
And give strength to your bones;
And you will be like a watered
garden,
And like a spring of water whose
waters do not fail.
And those from among you will
rebuild the ancient ruins;
You will raise up the age-old
foundations;
And you will be called the repairer
of the breach,
The restorer of the streets in which
to dwell.*

Isaiah 58:6–12

I don't know of a clearer passage of Scripture than Isaiah's words on the subject of compassion. Nor do I know of a better way to identify those who do the Good Samaritan work than "repairers of the breach" and "restorers of the streets."

Enough of words! This needy old world has heard such things before. What it longs for is action. Repairers and restorers at work . . . in the trenches . . . doing the things that give us the right to bear the name "Christian." And in the event you grow weary and your resolve to be different starts to wear thin, remember this:

OTHERS WILL NOT CARE HOW MUCH YOU KNOW UNTIL THEY KNOW HOW MUCH YOU CARE.

NOTES

1. A statement made by Dr. Carl F. H. Henry in a speech at the National Religious Broadcasters Convention in Washington, D.C. in January, 1983. Dr. Henry's source for the Niebuhr story was Dr. Ben Armstrong of NRB.

2. William M. Fletcher, The Second Greatest Commandment, (Colorado Springs, CO: NavPress, 1983), pp. 57–58.

3. Walter Tubbs, "Beyond Perls," *Journal of Humanistic Psychology,* vol. 12, no. 2 (1972), p. 5. Reprinted by permission of Saga Publications, Inc.

4. From the book, *Glad To Be Me*, edited by Dov Peretz Elkins, © 1976 by Prentice-Hall, Inc., pp. 28, 29.

Published by Prentice-Hall, Inc.
Englewood Cliffs, NJ 07632.

5. Jess Moody, *Quote-Unquote,* Lloyd Cory, ed. (Wheaton, IL: Victor Books, a division of SP Publications, Inc., 1977), p. 66.

6. Ruth Harms Calkin, *Tell Me Again, Lord, I Forget* (Elgin, IL: David C. Cook Publishing Co., 1974), p. 14. Used by permission of the author.

7. Jeremy C. Jackson, *No Other Foundation* (Westchester, IL: Cornerstone Books, 1980), p. 283.

8. Michael Quoist, quoted by William M. Fletcher in *The Second Greatest Commandment* (Colorado Springs, CO: NavPress, 1984), p. 43.

ABOUT THE AUTHOR

Ordained into the gospel ministry in 1963, Dr. Charles R. Swindoll has developed a popular expository pulpit style characterized by a clear and accurate presentation of Scripture, with a marked emphasis on the practical application of the Bible to everyday living, making God's truths a reality in the lives of hurting people.

Raised in Houston, Texas, and having originally pursued a career in engineering, Dr. Swindoll entered Dallas Theological Seminary in 1959 and graduated four years later with honors. In June 1977 an honorary doctor of divinity degree was conferred on him by Talbot Theological Seminary in La Mirada, California.

Since 1971 Dr. Swindoll has been senior pastor at the First Evangelical Free Church of Fullerton, California.

Currently, Dr. Swindoll's ministry is shared internationally through an extensive cassette tape distribution and a thirty-minute daily radio broadcast—"Insight for Living"—now being aired more than seven hundred times each day worldwide. "Insight for Living" received the prestigious Award of Merit from National

Religious Broadcasters for the outstanding religious broadcast in 1982.

A growing list of Dr. Swindoll's published works include the Christian film, *People of Refuge;* a six-message film series, *Strengthening Your Grip;* and more than fourteen books, among which are *Dropping Your Guard; Strengthening Your Grip; Improving Your Serve; Strike the Original Match;* and *Three Steps Forward, Two Steps Back.* Also available are sixteen booklets: *Anger, Attitudes, Commitment, Demonism, Destiny, Divorce, Eternal Security, God's Will, Hope, Integrity, Leisure, Sensuality, Singleness, Stress, Tongues,* and *Woman.*

Dr. Swindoll and his wife, Cynthia, have four children—Curtis and Charissa (both married) and Colleen and Chuck (both students still living at home). The Swindolls reside in Fullerton, California.